STATISTICS

THINGS YOU SHOULD KNOW
(QUESTIONS AND ANSWERS)

By Rumi Michael Leigh

Introduction

I would like to thank you for purchasing this book, *"Statistics, things you should know (questions and answers)"*.

This book will help you understand, revise, and have a good general knowledge and understanding of the basics of statistics.

I hope you enjoy it!

Table of Contents

4

Part 1

1.

What is statistics?

Statistics can be described as data facts.

2.

What is the field of statistics?

The field of statistics is the collection and analyses of data.

3.

Can statistics help us make decisions?

Yes, statistics can help us make decisions.

4.

Are there different types of statistics?

Yes, there are different types of statistics.

5.

What is descriptive statistics?

Descriptive statistics describes the information on a data.

6.

What is inferential statistics?

Inferential statistics leads to conclusions based on data.

7.

What is a hypothesis?

A hypothesis is a guess or a supposition.

8.

What is null?

Null signifies nothing.

9.

What is a null hypothesis?

A null hypothesis is a statistical hypothesis that suggests that there is no effect between groups or variables.

10.

What is the alternative hypothesis?

The alternative hypothesis is what you think is the true state of the population, and it's what you are trying to prove with your statistical test. It represents the opposite of the null hypothesis and represents what you expect to observe if the null hypothesis is false.

11.

What are null results?

Null results can be defined as results that do not support the hypothesis.

Part 2

1.

What is the mean?

The mean is the sum of numbers in a data set divided by the number of data points.

2.

The mean is also called?

The mean is also called the average.

3.

If John has 50 dollars and Sarah has 70 dollars, what is the mean?

The mean is (50+70)/2 = 60. So, the mean is 60

4.

What is the median?

The median is the middle number in a set of data from the smallest number to the largest number.

5.

What is the median of the following numbers: 1,3,5,6?

The median of the following numbers is 4 because (3+5)/2 = 4

6.

What is the median of the following numbers: 1,3,5,6,8?

The median of the following numbers is 5

7.

What is the mode?

The mode is the most popular value in a data.

8.

What is the mode of the following set of numbers: 1,5,7,5,8,12,12,13,2,5,8,1,5?

So, the mode of the following set of numbers is 5. This is so because, 5 appeared four times.

9.

Can there be more than one mode in a set of data?

Yes, there can be more than one mode in a set of data.

Part 3

1.

What is quantitative data?

Quantitative data is data with numerical value.

2.

What is categorical data?

Categorical data is data stored in categories.

3.

What is statistical measures of spread?

Statistical measures of spread shows how data is spread around the middle.

4.

Statistical measures of spread could also be called?

Statistical measures of spread could also be called dispersion.

5.

What is a distribution?

A distribution is how often each value occurs in a data set.

6.

What is Kurtosis?

Kurtosis is a measure of how the distribution of a set of values deviates from the normal (bell-shaped) distribution.

7.

Can Kurtosis be positive or negative?

Yes, Kurtosis can be positive or negative.

8.

How is positive Kurtosis?

Positive Kurtosis indicates a more peaked distribution.

9.

How is negative Kurtosis?

Negative Kurtosis indicates a flatter distribution.

10.

Normal distribution is also called?

Normal distribution is also called Gaussian distribution.

11.

What is binomial distribution?

Binomial distribution is the probability of having only two possible results.

12.

What is the Bernoulli distribution?

The Bernoulli distribution is the probability of getting a success or failure.

13.

What is Geometric distribution?

Geometric distribution is a discrete probability distribution that models counting the number of failures before the first success in a sequence of repeated independent trials with a fixed probability of success.

14.

What is T-distribution?

T-distribution is a distribution normally used for small sample sizes.

15.

Is a T-distribution a type of normal distribution?

Yes, a T-distribution is a type of normal distribution.

16.

A T-distribution is also called?

A T-distribution is also called Student's T-Distribution.

Part 4

1.

What is the interquartile range?

The interquartile range is the spread of the middle 50% of a data.

2.

Does the interquartile range take into consideration extreme values?

No, the interquartile range does not take into consideration extreme values.

3.

What is deviation?

Deviation is the difference from each point of the mean.

4.

What is the standard deviation?

The standard deviation is the square root of the variance.

5.

What does the variance show in a data?

The variance shows the variability in a data.

6.

What are the units of variants?

The units of variants are squared units.

7.

What is regression coefficient?

Regression coefficient measures the relationship between variables.

8.

What is correlation?

Correlation shows the relationship between variables.

9.

What is positive correlation?

Positive correlation is the relationship between variables that move in the same direction.

10.

What is negative correlation?

Negative correlation is the relationship between variables that do not move in the same direction.

Part 5

1.

What is causation?

Causation is what causes something, a change, etc.

2.

Does correlation always equal causation?

No, correlation does not always equal causation.

3.

What is spurious correlation?

Spurious correlation is a false relationship between two variables that is caused by a hidden factor, and not by any direct relationship between the variables themselves.

4.

What is empirical probability?

Empirical probability is what is observed in actual data.

5.

What is theoretical probability?

Theoretical probability is probability based on an event happening.

6.

What is conditional probability?

Conditional probability is the probability of an event to occur based on a previous event.

7.

What is a P-value?

P-value is the probability value that confirms or rejects a null hypothesis.

8.

What is statistical power?

Statistical power is the probability of detecting an effect if there is really an effect.

9.

What is the effect size?

The effect size is the distance between the mean of two distributions. It is a quantitative measure of the strength of the relationship between two variables in a given population.

10.

What is Bayesian statistics?

Bayesian statistics is when probability is used in statistical problems.

11.

Is Bayesian statistics usually objective?

No, Bayesian statistics is not usually objective because it contains beliefs.

Part 6

1.

What is the general linear model?

The general linear model is a framework that incorporates different statistical models.

2.

What are the main types of general linear model?

The main types of general linear model are the regression models, ANOVA, and ANCOVA.

3.

What is a regression line?

A regression line is a straight line that tries to connect all the data points.

4.

What are regressions?

Regressions aid in the analysis of two continuous variables.

5.

What is logistic regression?

Logistic regression is a type of regression analysis that is used to model the relationship between a set of predictor variables and a binary response variable.

6.

What is ANOVA?

ANOVA is the analysis of variance.

7.

What is factorial ANOVA?

Factorial ANOVA is a way to study the effects of more than one variable on a particular outcome at the same time.

8.

What is ANCOVA?

ANCOVA is the analysis of covariance.

Part 7

1.

What is an outlier?

An outlier is an abnormal data point compared to the other data points.

2.

What is a bias in data?

A bias is an error in data due to an underestimation or an overestimation of an element in a data.

3.

What is a biased question?

A biased question is a question asked in such a way that influences the answer to the question.

4.

What is response bias?

Response bias is an inaccurate response to a question due to influencing factors.

5.

What is standard error?

Standard error is the measurement of variability or uncertainty in an estimate based on a sample.

6.

What is a type 1 error?

A type 1 error is the rejection of the null hypothesis when it is true.

7.

Are type 1 errors false positives?

Yes, type 1 errors are false positives.

8.

Are type 2 errors false negatives?

Yes, type 2 errors are false negatives.

9.

What is type 2 error?

Type 2 error is when the null hypothesis is not rejected when it is false.

10.

What is the family wise error rate?

The family wise error rate is a way of controlling the probability of making incorrect conclusions when testing multiple ideas or relationships at the same time.

Part 8

1.

What is a control treatment?

A control treatment is when there is no actual treatment.

2.

What is a single-blind study?

A single blind study is where the people who are receiving the treatment don't know which treatment they are receiving. The treatment is only known by the researcher.

3.

What is a double-blind study?

A double-blind study is a study where the people who are receiving the treatment and the researchers don't know which treatment the subjects are receiving.

4.

What is an in-vitro study?

An in-vitro study is a scientific research performed in a laboratory.

5.

What is stratified random sampling?

Stratified random sampling is a way of dividing a population into subgroups and then randomly selecting a sample from each subgroup to ensure that the sample accurately represents the diversity within the population.

6.

What is cluster sampling?

In cluster sampling, the population is divided into separate groups called clusters.

7.

What are clusters?

Clusters are groups of data points or objects that are similar to one another and dissimilar to other data points or objects.

8.

What is snowball sampling?

Snowball sampling is when subjects are selected and then asked to recruit new subjects.

9.

What is a classifier?

A classifier classifies a group.

10.

What is a census?

A census is a survey that uses a whole population as a sample.

11.

What is linear discriminant analysis?

Linear discriminant analysis is a statistical technique used for classifying objects into one of several predefined categories or classes.

Part 9

1.

What is a percentile?

A percentile tells you what percent of the values are lower than a particular value in a set of data.

2.

What is big data?

Big data is a large amount of data.

3.

What is statistical inference?

Statistical inference is making conclusions from a data by analyzing the data.

4.

What is a confidence interval?

A confidence interval is a range of estimated plausible values based on observations.

5.

What are degrees of freedom?

Degrees of freedom is the number of independent values available to us in our data.

6.

What is critical value?

Critical value is the value that helps to find the margin of error in a set of data.

7.

What is replication?

Replication is repeating studies in order to confirm results.

Part 10

1.

What is a z-score?

A z-score shows the position of the score in a normal distribution.

2.

A z-score is also called?

A z-score is also called a standard score.

3.

What are T-tests?

T-tests compare the means of two set of data in order to see if the differences are statistically significant.

4.

What is a Chi-Square test?

A Chi-Square test is a statistical hypothesis test that enables the comparison between observed and expected results.

5.

What are the main ways Chi-Square test is used?

The main ways Chi-square test is used are: Goodness of fit test, Test of independence, and Test of Homogeneity.

6.

What is Goodness of fit test?

Goodness of fit test is a statistical method used to check how well a model fits a data

7.

What is test of independence?

Test of independence is a test that determines if one variable is independent or not of another variable.

8.

What is the test of Homogeneity?

The test of Homogeneity determines if different distributions are similar to one another.

9.

What is the F-test?

The F-test is a statistical test that shows how data fits a distribution.

10.

What is an omnibus test?

An omnibus test is a statistical test that contains several items and/or groups.

Part 11

1.

What is a continuous variable?

A continuous variable is a type of variable in mathematics and statistics that can take on any value within a specific range, rather than only certain defined values.

2.

Give examples of continuous variables.

Examples of continuous variables are temperature, length, height, income, time, etc.

3.

What are categorical variables?

Categorical variables are characteristics that can't be quantified.

4.

Categorical variables are also called?

Categorical variables are also called qualitative variables.

5.

Give examples of categorical variables.

Examples of categorical variables are age group, educational level, gender, etc.

6.

What is dimensionality reduction?

Dimensionality reduction is the reduction of the number of variables.

7.

What is Eta squared?

Eta squared is a way of quantifying the strength of the relationship between two variables. Eta squared is expressed as a value between 0 and 1. Values closer to 1 indicate strong relationship, and values closer to 0 indicate a weak relationship.

8.

What is an interaction plot?

An interaction plot is a graph that helps you see how two or more variables interact with each other to affect a particular outcome.

9.

What is a significant effect?

A significant effect means that there is a real relationship between two variables, and that the relationship is unlikely to be due to random chance.

10.

Is an interaction a significant effect?

Yes, an interaction is a significant effect.

11.

What is a main effect?

A main effect is the impact of a single factor on an outcome independent of any other factors that might also be present.

12.

What are log odds?

Log odds is a way of expressing the probability of an event happening (such as a yes/no event) as a number that ranges from negative infinity to positive infinity.

Conclusion

Thank you once again for purchasing this book. I hope it has helped you in your journey to understand the basics of statistics.

Please, if you learnt something from this book, I would like you to leave a review. It'd be appreciated.

Thank you.